3-digit numbers

Choose one stereo and one pair of headphones.

Write the total.

Do this 10 times.

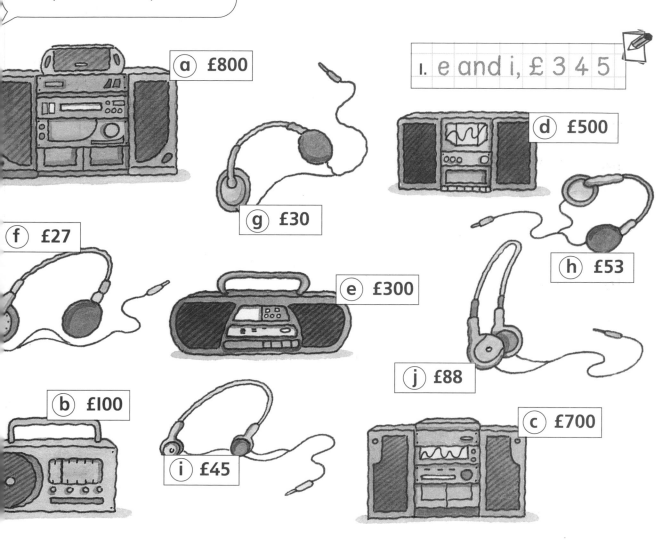

a £800

I. e and i, £ 3 4 5

d £500

g £30

f £27

h £53

e £300

j £88

b £100

c £700

i £45

Write each number in figures.

II. 3 6 8

11 Three hundred and sixty-eight

12 Four hundred and fifty-six

13 Two hundred and twenty-one

14 Eight hundred and ninety-nine

15 Five hundred and thirty-three

16 Six hundred and forty-two

17 Seven hundred and seventy-seven

3-digit numbers

Write how many
hundreds, tens and units.

1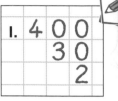
432

	4	0	0
1.		3	0
			2

2   748

3   691

4   820

5   506

6   299

7   144

8   307

9   916

10   333

11   808

12   485

13   750

Use number
cards 2, 5, 7, 9.

Make 4 numbers
with 9:

Number cards
(2, 5, 7, 9)

14   in the hundreds place

14.	7	9	5	2	,	5	9	2	7	,

15   in the tens place   16   in the thousands place   17   in the units place

4-digit numbers

> Choose 4 piles of bricks, one red, one blue, one yellow, one green.

> Write how many bricks in total.

> Do this 10 times.

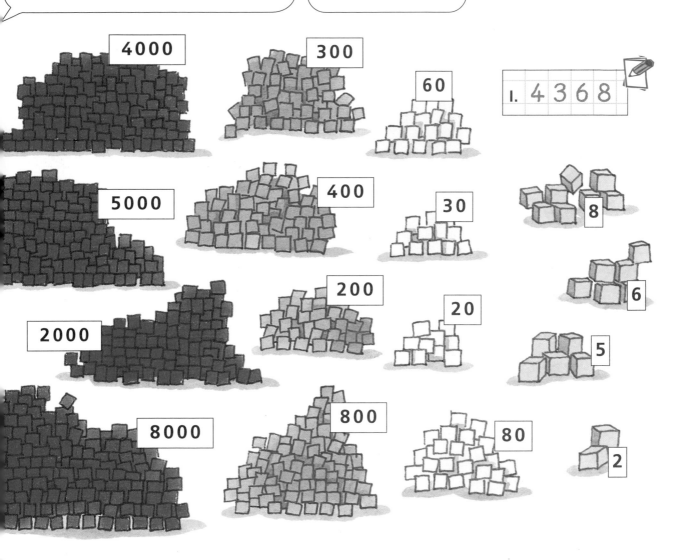

4000   300   60

I. 4 3 6 8

5000   400   30   8

2000   200   20   6

  5

8000   800   80   2

> Write each number in figures.

11 Four thousand, six hundred and twenty-one

11. 4 6 2 1

12 Six thousand, two hundred and forty

13 Nine thousand, two hundred and seven

14 Three thousand and thirty-six

15 Two thousand and twenty

16 Five thousand, five hundred and eighty-one

17 Seven thousand, six hundred and five

4-digit numbers

Write the position of each flag.

a. | 2 | 0 | 4 | 0

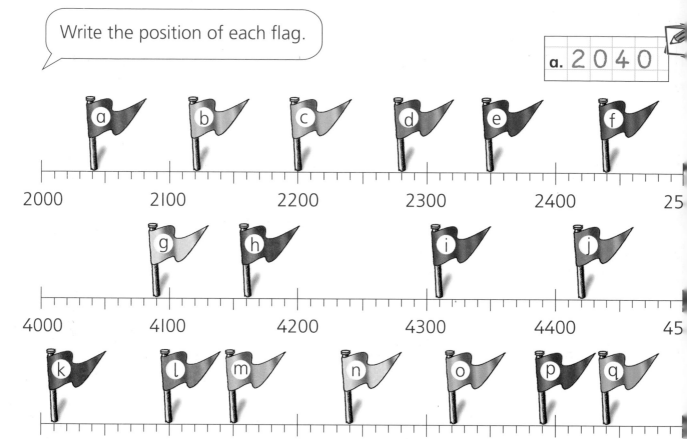

2000   2100   2200   2300   2400   25

4000   4100   4200   4300   4400   45

7500   7600   7700   7800   7900   80

Write the value of the <u>red</u> digit in each number.

1   7<u>2</u>60

1. | 2 | 0 | 0

2   154<u>3</u>   3   <u>2</u>486   4   93<u>7</u>2   5   <u>6</u>951

6   5<u>7</u>39   7   32<u>9</u>4   8   462<u>5</u>   9   <u>8</u>835

Write each number in words.

10   1268

10. one thousand, two hundred and sixty-eight

11   5943   12   7561   13   9797   14   2846

6

4-digit numbers

Write < or > each time.

1   1425 is less than 6874

1. $1\;4\;2\;5 < 6\;8\;7\;4$

2   5216 is more than 3318

3   2864 is more than 1524

10 < 15

is less than

4   1725 is less than 5692

5   1843 is more than 1685

28 > 20

is more than

6   7772 is less than 7785

7   8961 is more than 6891

8   9073 is more than 8982

9   9065 is less than 9102

10   2863 is more than 1052

11   2821 is less than 2921

12   5043 is less than 5403

13   3916 is more than 3816

Write < or > each time.

14   2804, 1734

14. $2\;8\;0\;4 > 1\;7\;3\;4$

15   1826, 5873

16   3205, 2305

17   8025, 8205

18   7510, 7150

19   4128, 4218

20   1104, 1105

21   9248, 9428

22   6909, 6990

23   3151, 5126

5-digit numbers

Write the total for each plane.

1. | 5 | 1 | , | 1 | 2 | 4 |

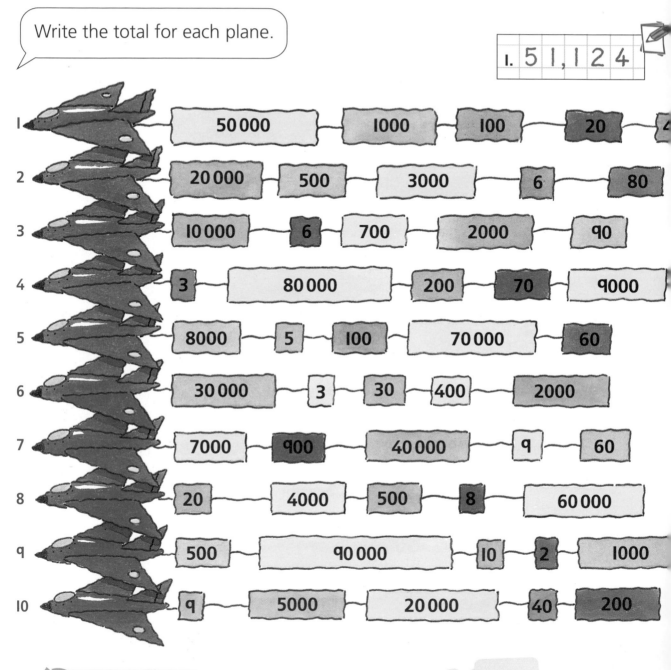

1. 50 000 — 1000 — 100 — 20 — 4

2. 20 000 — 500 — 3000 — 6 — 80

3. 10 000 — 6 — 700 — 2000 — 90

4. 3 — 80 000 — 200 — 70 — 9000

5. 8000 — 5 — 100 — 70 000 — 60

6. 30 000 — 3 — 30 — 400 — 2000

7. 7000 — 900 — 40 000 — 9 — 60

8. 20 — 4000 — 500 — 8 — 60 000

9. 500 — 90 000 — 10 — 2 — 1000

10. 9 — 5000 — 20 000 — 40 — 200

Explore

Use these number cards to make different 5-digit numbers.

Make the nearest number you can to 10 000, 20 000, 30 000, ... 90 000.

Rounding

Round each number to the nearest ten and the nearest hundred.

a. 2 8 4 mm → 2 8 0 mm
2 8 4 mm → 3 0 0 mm

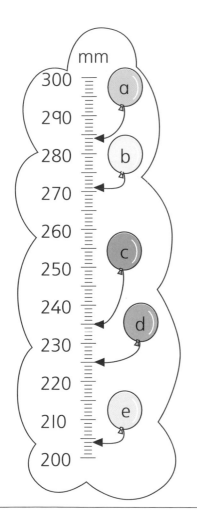

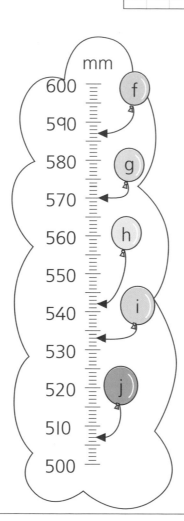

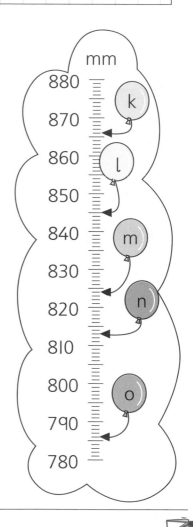

Round each amount to the nearest £10 and the nearest £100.

£363

1. £ 3 6 3 → £ 3 6 0
£ 3 6 3 → £ 4 0 0

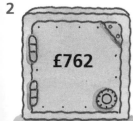

£762

£910

£449

£321

£741

9

Rounding

Round each number to the nearest ten and the nearest hundred.

1

1.	1	8	4	→	1 8 0
	1	8	4	→	2 0 0

2

3

4

5

6

7

8

9

10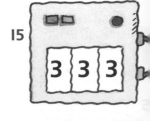

Round each number to the nearest ten and the nearest hundred.

11  3 2 1

11.	3	2	1	→	3 2 0
	3	2	1	→	3 0 0

12  4 4 0

13 6 4 8

14 5 7 9

15 3 3 3

16 2 8 2

17 1 4 3

18 7 9 1

19 8 2 6

Rounding

Round each number to the nearest ten and the nearest hundred.

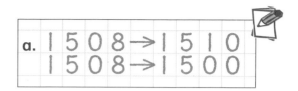

a. 1508 → 1510
   1508 → 1500

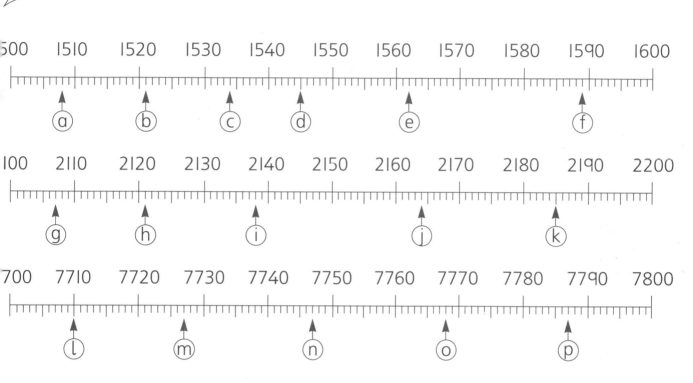

Round each length to the nearest ten and the nearest hundred.

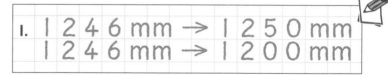

I. 1246 mm → 1250 mm
   1246 mm → 1200 mm

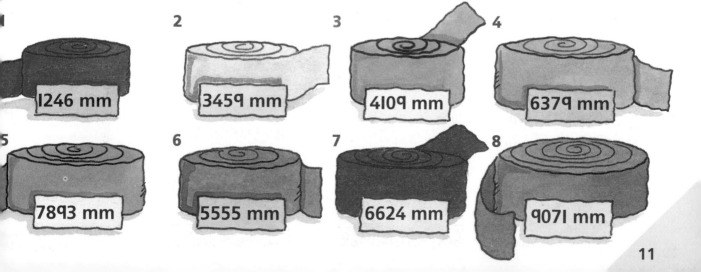

1 1246 mm
2 3459 mm
3 4109 mm
4 6379 mm
5 7893 mm
6 5555 mm
7 6624 mm
8 9071 mm

Rounding

The numbers show how many light-years each star is from the Sun.

Round each to the nearest ten and the nearest hundred.

a.	9	2	8	1	→	9	2	8	0
	9	2	8	1	→	9	3	0	0

ⓒ 7378

ⓗ 2236

ⓕ 4864

ⓑ 8645

Sun

ⓓ 6432

ⓖ 3584

ⓘ 8555

ⓔ 5199

ⓙ 4218

ⓐ 9281

 **Explore**

How many numbers can you find that have 5000 as their nearest thousand?

Their digits must add up to 20.

5000

Adding

> Copy and complete.

I $7 + 6 + 3 =$

I. $7 + 6 + 3 = 16$

2   $8 + 7 + 2 =$ 3 $9 + 8 + 1 =$

> Look for 10s

4   $4 + 5 + 6 =$ 5 $3 + 9 + 7 =$ 6 $5 + 8 + 5 + 1 =$

7   $11 + 7 + 3 + 2 =$ 8 $6 + 12 + 4 + 1 =$ 9 $1 + 13 + 9 + 2 =$

> Choose 3 stickers, and find the total.

> Do this 10 times.

10. $6p + 8p + 2p = 16p$

Aston Villa 6p

Manchester United 7p

Leeds United 3p

Southampton F.C. 4p

Arsenal F.C. 9p

Glasgow Rangers 8p

Liverpool F.C. 5p

Newcastle United 2p

> Choose 4 stickers, and find the total.

> Do this 5 times.

20. $6p + 7p + 3p + 4p = 20p$

13

Adding

Copy and complete.

1. $8 + 3 + 6 =$

1. $8 + 3 + 6 = 17$

2. $9 + 3 + 6 =$

3. $7 + 2 + 8 =$

4. $6 + 5 + 8 =$

5. $5 + 8 + 9 =$

6. $3 + 7 + 8 =$

7. $9 + 4 + 8 =$

8. $6 + 7 + 9 =$

9. $12 + 3 + 8 =$

10. $13 + 6 + 7 =$

Each cake goes up by 9p.

Write the new prices.

11. $12p + 9p = 21p$

11  12p

12  28p

13 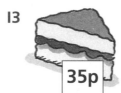 35p

14  23p

15 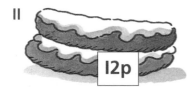 17p

16  25p

17  39p

18  22p

---

Choose 2 blue stamps and 2 red stamps.

Write the total.

Do this 5 times.

19. $12p + 9p + 3p + 7p = 31p$

3p 2p 6p 11p 7p 9p 12p 4p 8p

Adding

Write how many red and blue squares in each strip.

1

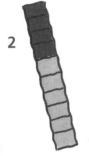 2

 3

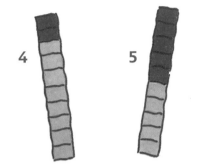 4 5

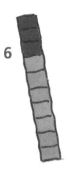 6

1

1. $1 + 9 = 10$

Write how many pink and yellow squares in each grid.

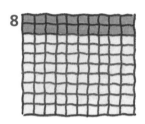 8

8. $20 + 80 = 100$

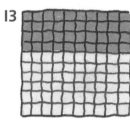 9

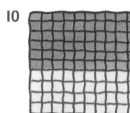 10

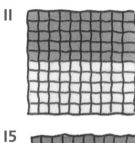 11

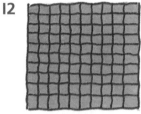 12

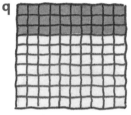 13

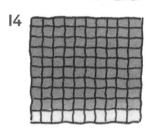 14

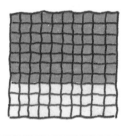 15

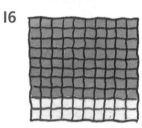 16

Write the missing numbers.

17  + 30 = 100

17. $70 + 30 = 100$

18  + 60 = 100

19 + 10 = 100

20 + 40 = 100

21 80 +  = 100

22 50 + = 100

23 20 +  = 100

15

Adding to 100

Write how many blue and yellow squares in each grid.

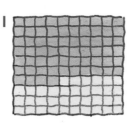

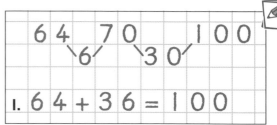

1. $64 + 36 = 100$

2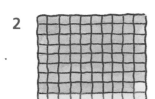

3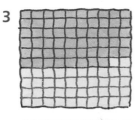

4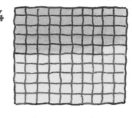

5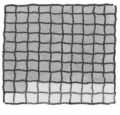

6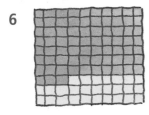

7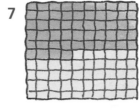

8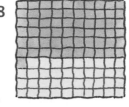

q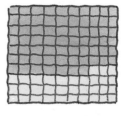

10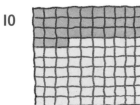

ll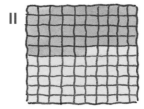

12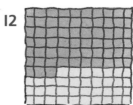

13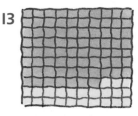

14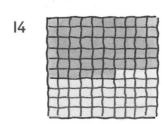

15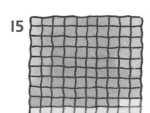

16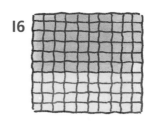

17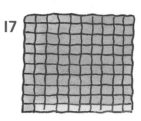

Write the missing numbers.

18   ✿ $+ 62 = 100$

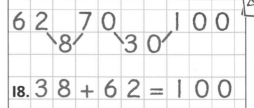

18. $38 + 62 = 100$

19 $84 +$ ✿ $= 100$

20   ✿ $+ 76 = 100$

21 $31 +$ ✿ $= 100$

22   ✿ $+ 71 = 100$

23 $28 +$ ✿ $= 100$

24 $49 +$ ✿ $= 100$

25   ✿ $+ 35 = 100$

26 $17 +$ ✿ $= 100$

Adding to 100

> Each video is 100 minutes long.

> Write how many minutes to go.

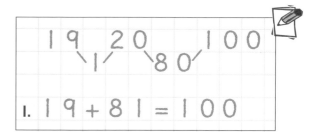

1. $19 + 81 = 100$

1. :19	2. :23	3. :42
4. :51	5. :37	6. :08
7. :28	8. :15	9. :54

> Write pairs that add up to 100.

10. $62 + 38 = 100$

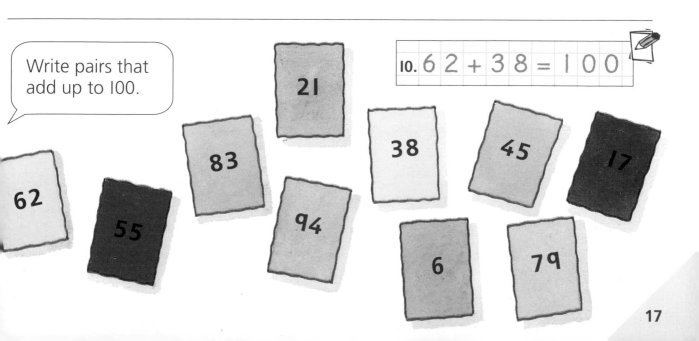

21 83 38 45 17 62 55 94 6 79

17

Write how many degrees to reach 100.

1. $6 1 + 3 9 = 1 0 0$

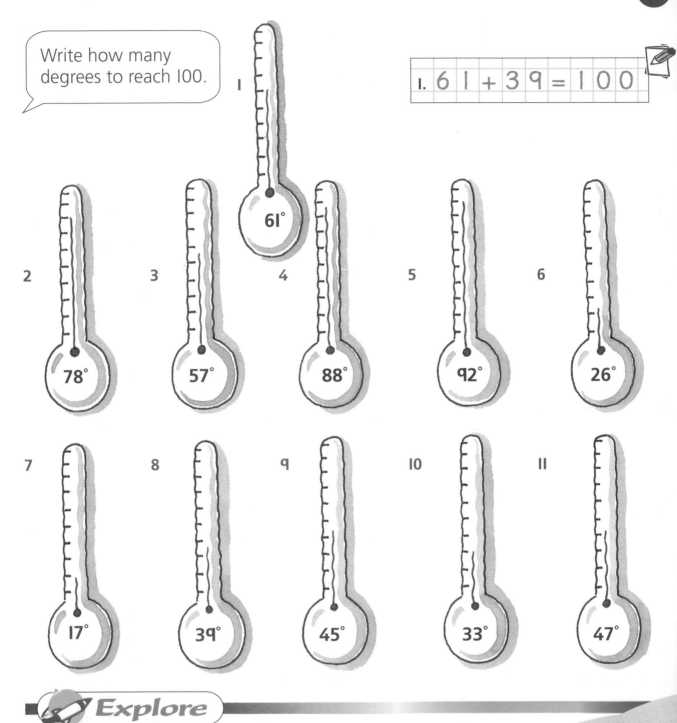

1 (thermometer) 61°

2 78°

3 57°

4 88°

5 92°

6 26°

7 17°

8 39°

9 45°

10 33°

11 47°

Explore

Write pairs of numbers that add up to 100.

How many can you write where all the digits are odd?

Adding

Copy and complete.

Estimate first.

```
1   H T U
    3 8 0
  + 2 4 0
  _____
```

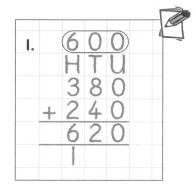

```
I.   (6 0 0)
      H T U
      3 8 0
    + 2 4 0
    _____
      6 2 0
      1
```

```
2   H T U
    4 9 0
  + 2 3 0
  _____
```

```
3   H T U
    5 7 0
  + 2 9 0
  _____
```

```
4   H T U
    6 6 0
  + 3 2 0
  _____
```

```
5   H T U
    7 7 0
  + 3 9 0
  _____
```

```
6   H T U
    7 5 0
  + 2 4 0
  _____
```

```
7   H T U
    3 9 0
  + 4 8 0
  _____
```

```
8   H T U
    4 7 0
  + 3 4 0
  _____
```

```
9   H T U
    6 8 0
  + 3 8 0
  _____
```

```
10  H T U
    7 9 0
  + 4 6 0
  _____
```

```
11  H T U
    8 2 0
  + 7 8 0
  _____
```

```
12  H T U
    5 1 0
  + 3 7 0
  _____
```

```
13  H T U
    8 3 0
  + 1 1 0
  _____
```

Add each pink number to each blue number.

Estimate first.

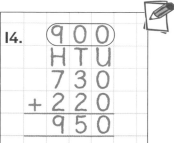

```
14.  (9 0 0)
      H T U
      7 3 0
    + 2 2 0
    _____
      9 5 0
```

220

170

660

730

380

840

Adding

Copy and complete.

Estimate first.

```
   Th H  T  U
    5  7  0  0
 +  2  1  0  0
 _____
```

1.
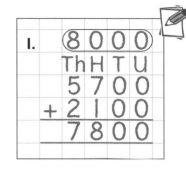
```
     8 0 0 0
   Th H T U
    5 7 0 0
  + 2 1 0 0
   _____
    7 8 0 0
```

2
```
   Th H  T  U
    3  9  0  0
 +  6  8  0  0
 _____
```

3
```
   Th H  T  U
    4  8  0  0
 +  2  9  0  0
 _____
```

4
```
   Th H  T  U
    7  2  0  0
 +  3  4  0  0
 _____
```

5
```
   Th H  T  U
    8  7  0  0
 +  3  2  0  0
 _____
```

6
```
   Th H  T  U
    4  9  0  0
 +  5  8  0  0
 _____
```

7
```
   Th H  T  U
    7  8  0  0
 +  6  9  0  0
 _____
```

8
```
   Th H  T  U
    8  1  0  0
 +  2  7  0  0
 _____
```

9
```
   Th H  T  U
    6  6  0  0
 +  3  4  0  0
 _____
```

Each cub's weight goes up by 1300 g.

Write the new weights.

10.
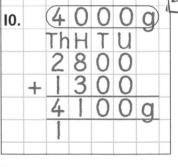
```
     4 0 0 0 g
   Th H T U
    2 8 0 0
  + 1 3 0 0
   _____
    4 1 0 0 g
      1
```

10

2800 g

11

1700 g

12

3900 g

13

2500 g

14

3600 g

15

4800 g

16

1200 g

20

Each runner goes another 1240 m.

Write the new distances.

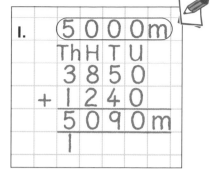

1. (5000m)
    Th H T U
       3 8 5 0
    + 1 2 4 0
       5 0 9 0 m
           1

1

3850 m

2

4870 m

3

5990 m

4

6120 m

5

7490 m

6

3980 m

7

2490 m

8

7770 m

9

2960 m

10

6330 m

 Explore

Look at this addition.

Each letter stands for a digit.

Find numbers to make the addition correct.

```
  c a t s
+ d o g s
---------
  m e s s
```

try
s = 0

21

0   5   10   15   20   25   30

Copy and complete.

1   15 – 9 =

1. | 1 | 5 | – | 9 | = | 6 |

2   13 – 5 =

3   11 – 6 =

Use the number line to help you.

4   23 – 17 =

5   17 – 8 =

6   12 – 4 =

7   25 – 16 =

8   14 – 7 =

9   22 – 15 =

Write how much is left if you spend 8p.

10   (10p) (1p) (1p)

10. | 1 | 2 | p | – | 8 | p | = | 4 | p |

11   (10p) (1p) (1p) (1p) (1p) (1p)

12   (10p) (1p) (1p) (10p) (1p)

13   (10p) (10p) (1p) (10p)

14   (10p) (10p) (1p) (5p)

15   (10p) (1p) (1p) (10p) (1p) (1p)

16   (10p) (10p) (1p) (1p) (10p) (10p)

17   (10p) (10p) (1p) (1p) (1p) (1p) (1p) (1p)

18   (10p) (1p) (1p) (1p) (1p)

Taking away

Copy and complete.

1
```
  H T U
  3 4 5
- 1 2 4
-------
```

```
1.  H T U
    3 4 5
  - 1 2 4
  -------
    2 2 1
```

2
```
  H T U
  7 8 0
- 3 1 0
-------
```

3
```
  H T U
  5 8 0
- 3 4 0
-------
```

4
```
  H T U
  6 4 0
- 4 3 0
-------
```

5
```
  H T U
  7 5 3
- 5 2 2
-------
```

6
```
  H T U
  8 2 9
- 4 1 7
-------
```

7
```
  H T U
  5 2 9
- 2 1 6
-------
```

8
```
  H T U
  2 5 6
- 1 3 2
-------
```

9
```
  H T U
  4 7 8
- 2 3 5
-------
```

Write how much change from £778 for each bicycle.

10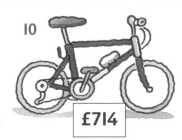

£714

```
10.  H T U
     7 7 8
   - 7 1 4
   -------
   £   6 4
```

11

£623

12

£333

13

£65

14

£236

15

£466

16

£545

17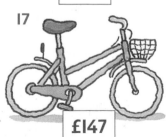

£147

18

£721

Taking away

The course is 878 m long.

Write how far each must go to finish.

a.

H	T	U
8	7	8
− 7	2	3
1	5	5 m

(a) 723 m

(b) 637 m

(c) 606 m

(d) 558 m

(e) 513 m

(f) 424 m

(g) 361 m

(h) 207 m

(i) 132 m

(j) 75 m

Take each pink number away from each blue number.

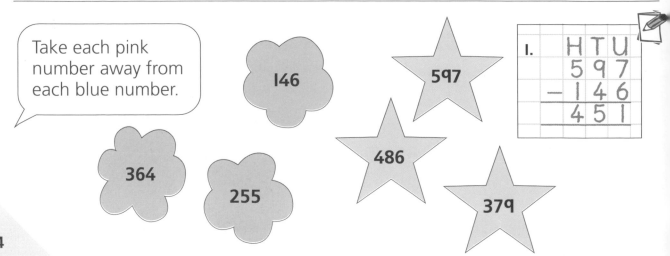

146

597

364

255

486

379

l.

H	T	U
5	9	7
− 1	4	6
4	5	1

Copy and complete.

1
```
Th H T U
   4 7 5 8
 - 2 3 1 4
 _____
```

```
     Th H T U
1.      4 7 5 8
      - 2 3 1 4
      _____
        2 4 4 4
```

2
```
Th H T U
   6 5 3 4
 - 2 3 1 2
 _____
```

3
```
Th H T U
   2 7 8 3
 - 1 4 5 0
 _____
```

4
```
Th H T U
   4 9 5 6
 - 1 4 2 0
 _____
```

5
```
Th H T U
   1 7 9 5
 - 1 2 6 1
 _____
```

6
```
Th H T U
   8 3 9 2
 - 4 1 5 2
 _____
```

7
```
Th H T U
   4 7 9 3
 - 2 3 5 2
 _____
```

8
```
Th H T U
   2 8 6 3
 - 1 1 4 1
 _____
```

9
```
Th H T U
   5 4 5 6
 - 4 1 3 5
 _____
```

10
```
Th H T U
   9 3 7 4
 - 6 2 5 1
 _____
```

11
```
Th H T U
   6 5 9 8
 - 3 4 7 2
 _____
```

12
```
Th H T U
   4 6 3 9
 - 1 4 1 8
 _____
```

13
```
Th H T U
   5 8 7 6
 - 2 5 4 2
 _____
```

 **Explore**

Use number cards 1, 3, 4, 5.

Make different 4-digit numbers and take them away from 7896.

What is the largest answer you can make?

What is the nearest answer to 2000, 3000, ... 6000?

25

Add to each number to make the next thousand.

a. $2200 + 800 = 3000$

a   b   c   d   e

2000   3000

f   g   h   i   j

5000   6000

k   l   m   n   o

7000   8000

Write how many points are needed for the next thousand.

1570   1600   2000
　　　　＼30／　　＼400／

l. $1570 + 430 = 2000$

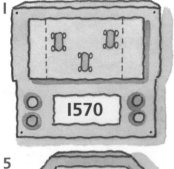
1 1570

2 2460

3 4350

4 2710

5 4680

6 3940

7 2030

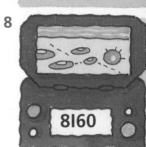
8 8160

The next thousand

How many people will make the next thousand in each stadium?

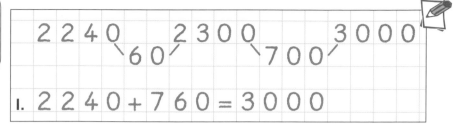

|2 2 4 0| | |2 3 0 0| | | |3 0 0 0|

\60/ \700/

1. 2 2 4 0 + 7 6 0 = 3 0 0 0

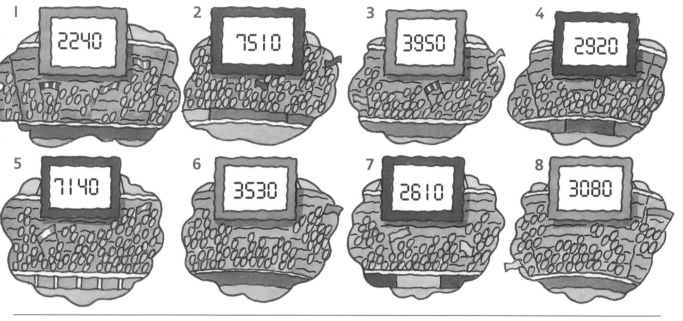

1	2	3	4
2240	7510	3950	2920

5	6	7	8
7140	3530	2610	3080

Write how many more miles to reach the next thousand.

|1 5 7 2| |1 5 8 0| | |1 6 0 0| |2 0 0 0|

\8/ \20/ \400/

q. 1 5 7 2 + 4 2 8 = 2 0 0 0

9. | 1 | 5 | 7 | 2 |

10. | 2 | 3 | 4 | 5 |

11. | 4 | 1 | 2 | 6 |

12. | 3 | 7 | 8 | 4 |

13. | 2 | 5 | 9 | 3 |

14. | 4 | 5 | 6 | 2 |

15. | 3 | 8 | 0 | 7 |

16. | 2 | 4 | 1 | 6 |

27

Write how much more money will make the next thousand pounds.

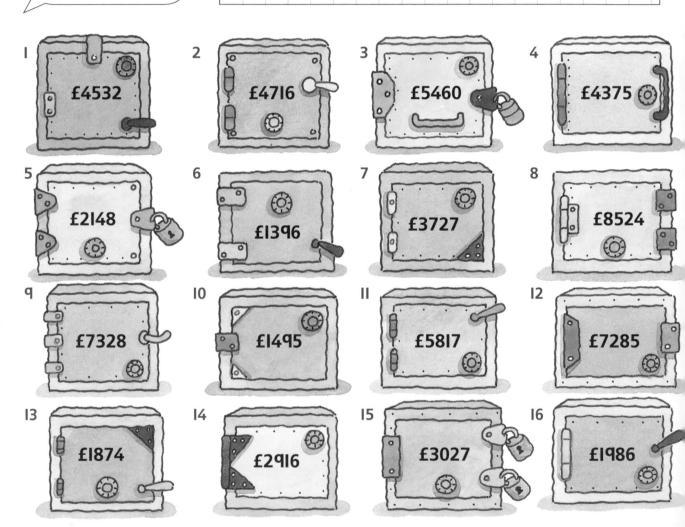

```
4 5 3 2    4 5 4 0    4 6 0 0    5 0 0 0
        \8/        \60/        \400/
```

1. £4 5 3 2 + £4 6 8 = £5 0 0 0

1	£4532
2	£4716
3	£5460
4	£4375
5	£2148
6	£1396
7	£3727
8	£8524
9	£7328
10	£1495
11	£5817
12	£7285
13	£1874
14	£2916
15	£3027
16	£1986

Explore

What goes with: 222 to make 2000?
333 to make 3000?
444 to make 4000?

Continue.

Can you see a pattern?

Taking away

Subtraction (Red strand)

N7

> Copy and complete.

1.
```
  H T U
  3 7 2
- 1 5 8
---------
```

1.
```
  H T U    (+2)    H T U
  3 7 2            3 7 4
- 1 5 8          - 1 6 0
                 --------
                   2 1 4
```

2.
```
  H T U
  4 8 1
- 1 3 9
```

3.
```
  H T U
  3 9 3
- 1 5 8
```

4.
```
  H T U
  5 6 4
- 2 4 7
```

5.
```
  H T U
  6 5 2
- 3 1 8
```

6.
```
  H T U
  4 7 5
- 1 3 9
```

7.
```
  H T U
  5 4 1
- 3 2 6
```

8.
```
  H T U
  7 8 3
- 4 5 8
```

9.
```
  H T U
  8 9 2
- 3 4 7
```

10.
```
  H T U
  3 2 5
- 2 1 7
```

11.
```
  H T U
  6 8 7
- 4 4 8
```

12.
```
  H T U
  4 2 8
- 2 7 2
```

12.
```
  H T U    (+8)    H T U    (+20)    H T U
  4 2 8            4 3 6             4 5 6
- 2 7 2          - 2 8 0           - 3 0 0
                                   --------
                                     1 5 6
```

13.
```
  H T U
  6 3 7
- 2 8 3
```

14.
```
  H T U
  5 1 8
- 1 9 4
```

15.
```
  H T U
  4 4 5
- 2 6 1
```

16.
```
  H T U
  7 3 6
- 3 9 2
```

17.
```
  H T U
  8 2 9
- 1 7 3
```

18.
```
  H T U
  9 5 4
- 6 8 2
```

19.
```
  H T U
  7 4 5
- 4 6 4
```

20.
```
  H T U
  6 2 8
- 3 8 3
```

21.
```
  H T U
  5 3 5
- 2 4 4
```

22.
```
  H T U
  6 6 8
- 4 7 3
```

29

Taking away

Copy and complete.

1.
```
  H T U
  3 7 2
- 1 5 8
───────
```

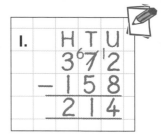

I.
```
   H T U
   3 6 7 1 2
 - 1   5 8
 ─────────
   2   1 4
```

2.
```
  H T U
  4 8 1
- 1 3 9
───────
```

3.
```
  H T U
  3 9 3
- 1 5 8
───────
```

4.
```
  H T U
  5 6 4
- 2 4 7
───────
```

5.
```
  H T U
  6 5 2
- 3 1 8
───────
```

6.
```
  H T U
  4 7 5
- 1 3 9
───────
```

7.
```
  H T U
  5 4 1
- 3 2 6
───────
```

8.
```
  H T U
  7 8 3
- 4 5 8
───────
```

9.
```
  H T U
  8 9 2
- 3 4 7
───────
```

10.
```
  H T U
  3 2 5
- 2 1 7
───────
```

11.
```
  H T U
  6 8 7
- 4 4 8
───────
```

Copy and complete.

12.
```
  H T U
  4 2 8
- 2 7 2
───────
```

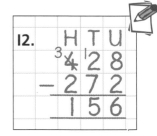

12.
```
   H T U
   3 4 1 2 8
 - 2   7 2
 ─────────
   1   5 6
```

13.
```
  H T U
  6 3 7
- 2 8 3
───────
```

14.
```
  H T U
  5 1 8
- 1 9 4
───────
```

15.
```
  H T U
  4 4 5
- 2 6 1
───────
```

16.
```
  H T U
  7 3 6
- 3 9 2
───────
```

17.
```
  H T U
  8 2 9
- 1 7 3
───────
```

18.
```
  H T U
  9 5 4
- 6 8 2
───────
```

19.
```
  H T U
  7 4 5
- 4 6 4
───────
```

20.
```
  H T U
  6 2 8
- 3 8 3
───────
```

21.
```
  H T U
  5 3 5
- 2 4 4
───────
```

22.
```
  H T U
  6 6 8
- 4 7 3
───────
```

Taking away

Write how many voted 'yes' in each school.

1
Three Stars
475 children
'no', 146

1.

	H	T	U
	4	7	5
−	1	4	6

2
St Mary's
542 children
'no', 227

3
Park Vale
483 children
'no', 238

4
692 children
'no', 335

5
Compton School
345 children
'no', 172

6
Castle Town
426 children
'no', 251

7
637 children
'no', 362

8
St John's
558 children
'no', 274

9
Cameron
472 children
'no', 238

10
Ribbon Valley
546 children
'no', 281

11
Oakfield
529 children
'no', 336

12
Pud Lane
382 children
'no', 156

13
225 children
'no', 133

Write the difference between the numbers of 'yes' and 'no' votes in each school.

Three Stars
'no', 146
'yes', 329

14.

	H	T	U
	3	2	9
−	1	4	6

31

Taking away

Write the new amounts.

1. 450 ml drinks 185 ml

	H	T	U
1.	4	5	0
−	1	8	5

_____ ml

2. 280 ml drinks 156 ml

3. 314 ml drinks 135 ml

4. 562 ml drinks 127 ml

5. 735 ml drinks 249 ml

6. 540 ml drinks 325 ml

7. 630 ml drinks 413 ml

8. 420 ml drinks 275 ml

9. 445 ml drinks 260 ml

10. 625 ml drinks 339 ml

11. 342 ml drinks 225 ml

12. 525 ml drinks 348 ml

13. 463 ml drinks 172 ml

Explore

Use number cards 1, 2, 4, 6, 7, 9.

Make two 3-digit numbers.

Take the smaller away from the larger.

How many subtractions can you make with an answer of more than 750?

Taking away

Write how many boys are in each audience.

1
4528 children
1341 girls

	Th	H	T	U
I.	4	5	2	8
−	1	3	4	1

2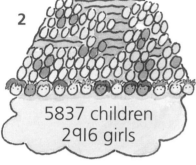
5837 children
2916 girls

3
4930 children
2340 girls

4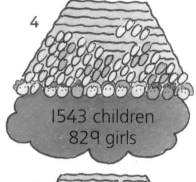
1543 children
829 girls

5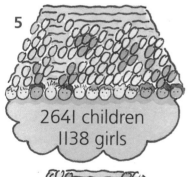
2641 children
1138 girls

6
3527 children
2138 girls

7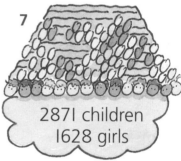
2871 children
1628 girls

8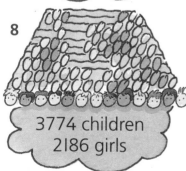
3774 children
2186 girls

9
4352 children
2168 girls

10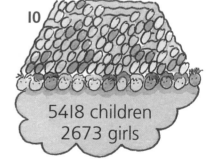
5418 children
2673 girls

Write the difference between the numbers of girls and boys in each audience.

1341 girls
3187 boys

	Th	H	T	U
II.	3	1	8	7
−	1	3	4	1

Multiplying

Write a multiplication for each number.

Use the grid to help you.

1. $3 \times 5 = 15$

	1	2	3	4	5	6	7	8	9	10
2	2	4	6	8	10	12	14	16	18	20
3	3	6	9	12	15	18	21	24	27	30
4	4	8	12	16	20	24	28	32	36	40
5	5	10	15	20	25	30	35	40	45	50
6	6	12	18	24	30	36	42	48	54	60
7	7	14	21	28	35	42	49	56	63	70
8	8	16	24	32	40	48	56	64	72	80
9	9	18	27	36	45	54	63	72	81	90
10	10	20	30	40	50	60	70	80	90	100

1 15 2 18 3 35

4 16 5 27 6 36

7 8 8 20 9 49

10 72 11 28 12 56

13 48 14 63 15 70

Copy and complete.

16   $4 \times 6 =$

16. $4 \times 6 = 24$

17   $3 \times 7 =$

18   $2 \times 9 =$

19   $5 \times 6 =$

20   $10 \times 3 =$

21   $3 \times 6 =$

22   $7 \times 8 =$

23   $9 \times 5 =$

24   $7 \times 4 =$

25   $5 \times 4 =$

26   $8 \times 8 =$

27   $7 \times 6 =$

28   $8 \times 6 =$

Multiplying

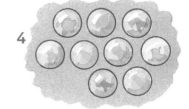

> Each marble costs 7p.

> Write the cost of each set.

1. $3 \times 7p = 21p$

1

2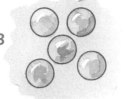

3

4

5

6

7

8

q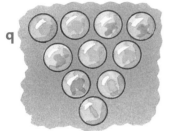

10

ll

12

> Write the cost of each set if each marble costs:

a **qp**

b **5p**

1a. $3 \times 9p = 27p$

1b. $3 \times 5p = 15p$

> Copy and complete the table.

in	3	5		
out	1 8			

in	3	5	l	7	0	6	2	q	4	8	10
out											

> Complete a new table for a ×4 machine.

> Complete a table for a ×8 machine.

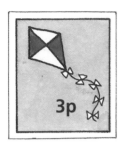 3p

 5p

 6p

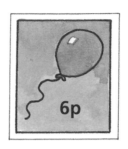 7p

 8p

> Write the cost of each set of stamps.

1

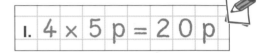
1. $4 \times 5p = 20p$

2
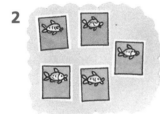

3
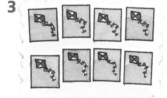

4

5
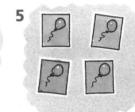

6

7

8

9

10

11

12

13

 **Explore**

Use number cards 4, 5, 6, 7, 8, 9.

Choose any two and multiply the numbers together.

How many different odd answers are possible?

How many different even answers are possible?

Multiplying

Write the missing numbers.

1   3 × 🌸 = 15

1. $3 \times 5 = 15$

2   4 × 🌸 = 28

3   5 × 🌸 = 20

4   7 × 🌸 = 42

5   🌸 × 8 = 24

6   🌸 × 9 = 45

7   7 × 🌸 = 21

8   10 × 🌸 = 50

9   🌸 × 6 = 54

10   🌸 × 5 = 40

11   7 × 🌸 = 56

12   🌸 × 9 = 36

13   🌸 × 4 = 24

14   8 × 🌸 = 48

15   🌸 × 4 = 16

16   6 × 🌸 = 36

Anu saves £3 a week.

Write how much she will have saved after:

17. $3 \times £3 = £9$

17   3 weeks

18   5 weeks

19   7 weeks

20   9 weeks

21   6 weeks

22   2 weeks

23   8 weeks

24   4 weeks

Write Anu's new totals if she saves:

a   £5 a week

17a. $3 \times £5 = £15$

b   £7 a week

c   £4 a week

d   £9 a week

Write the missing multiples.

1. 2, 4, 6, 8, 10,

1 | 2 | 4 | | 8 | | 12 | 14 | | 18 |

2 | 5 | | 15 | 20 | 25 | | | 40 | | 50

3 | 7 | 14 | 21 | | 35 | | 49 | | 63 |

4 | 4 | 8 | | 16 | | | 28 | | 36 | 40

5 | 6 | 12 | 18 | | 30 | | 42 | 48 | |

6 | 9 | 18 | | 36 | 45 | | 63 | 72 | | 90

7 | 8 | 16 | 24 | | 40 | | 56 | | 72 |

Write the next 5 multiples in each set.

1a. 22, 24,

Explore

These are the multiples of 5:

5 10 15 20 25 ...

Their units digits are:

5 0 5 0 5 ...

Explore patterns in the units digits
of other multiples.

Multiples

Write the next 5 multiples for each team.

1. 16, 20, 24,

1  Fours — 4, 8, 12

2  Sixes — 6, 12, 18

3  Sevens — 7, 14, 21

4  Nines — 9, 18, 27

5  Threes — 3, 6, 9

6  Eights — 8, 16, 24

7  Fives — 5, 10, 15

8  Elevens — 11, 22, 33

9  Twos — 2, 4, 6

Write the missing multiples.

10. 11, 22, 33,

10  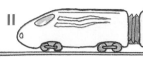 11, 22, [ ], 44, [ ], [ ], 77, [ ], [ ], 110

11   12, 24, 36, [ ], [ ], 72, [ ], [ ], 108, [ ]

12  15, 30, 45, [ ], [ ], 90, [ ], 120, [ ], [ ]

13 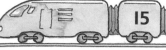      20, 40, [ ], 80, [ ], [ ], [ ], 160, [ ], 200

39

Multiples

Write all the numbers that have each bus number as a multiple.

1

6

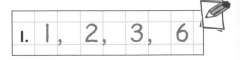

| 1. | 1, | 2, | 3, | 6 |

2

18

3

9

4

12

5

16

6

24

7

22

8

36

9

30

10

4

11

49

12

15

13

42

Explore

Choose two numbers, both less than 10, for example 3 and 5.

Write numbers that are multiples of both:
  15, 30, 45, 60, …

Write them all up to 100.

Try for different pairs of numbers.

3 and 5
15, 30, 45, 60, 75, 90
4 and 6
12, 24,

Dividing

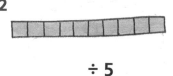

Write a division for each strip.

1 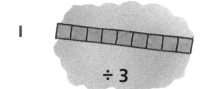÷ 3

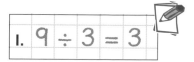
1. $9 \div 3 = 3$

2
÷ 5

3
÷ 3

4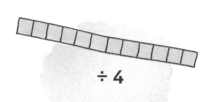
÷ 4

5
÷ 7

6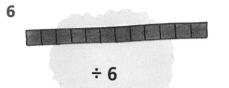
÷ 6

7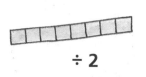
÷ 2

Copy and complete.

8 $24 \div 4 =$

8. $24 \div 4 = 6$

9 $18 \div 3 =$ **10** $35 \div 5 =$

11 $28 \div 4 =$ **12** $30 \div 10 =$

Use your fingers and tables lists to help you.

13 $54 \div 9 =$ **14** $40 \div 5 =$ **15** $63 \div 9 =$ **16** $32 \div 4 =$

17 $70 \div 10 =$ **18** $27 \div 3 =$ **19** $45 \div 9 =$ **20** $36 \div 4 =$

21 $24 \div 3 =$ **22** $16 \div 4 =$ **23** $25 \div 5 =$ **24** $81 \div 9 =$

25 $15 \div 3 =$ **26** $80 \div 10 =$ **27** $50 \div 5 =$ **28** $36 \div 6 =$

Write a list of multiples for each of these tables.

1 × 4

1. 4, 8, 12, 16,

2 × 6   3 × 7   4 × 8   5 × 5   6 × 9

Write how many:

7   6s in 42

7. 42 ÷ 6 = 7

8   3s in 24   9   4s in 28   10   7s in 35

11   8s in 56   12   3s in 18   13   8s in 32

14   4s in 36   15   7s in 21   16   5s in 45

17   10s in 50   18   2s in 16   19   8s in 64

20   7s in 49   21   9s in 81   22   6s in 54

23   4s in 16   24   7s in 42   25   4s in 24

26   3s in 21   27   5s in 40   28   8s in 48

Dividing

Write how many £5 notes you need to buy each item.

1  £35

I. $35 \div 5 = 7$

2  £40

3  £25

4  £10

5  £55

6  £45

7  £50

8 £5

9  £20

10  £30

11  £15

12  £65

13  £60

Write how many weeks until each child's birthday.

14  21 days

14. $21 \div 7 = 3$

15  63 days

16  56 days

17  49 days

18  28 days

19  42 days

20  14 days

21  35 days

22  70 days

Dividing

> Each egg-box holds 6 eggs

> How many egg-boxes are needed for each set?

1. $30 \div 6 = 5$

1
30 eggs

2
18 eggs

3
24 eggs

4
36 eggs

5
42 eggs

6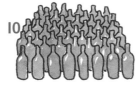
48 eggs

7
12 eggs

8
60 eggs

> Each box holds 9 bottles.

> Write how many boxes are needed for each set.

9. $18 \div 9 = 2$

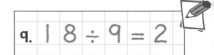

9
18 bottles

10
54 bottles

11
45 bottles

12
27 bottles

13
36 bottles

> Each crate holds 8 bottles.

> Write how many crates are needed for each set.

14. $16 \div 8 = 2$

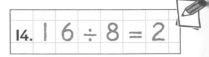

14
16 bottles

15
48 bottles

16
64 bottles

17
72 bottles

18
32 bottles

Dividing

Copy and complete.

1   5)42

1.   8 r 2
     5)4 2

Use tables lists
to help you.

2   4)23   3   6)50   4   7)50

5   8)27   6   5)54   7   9)64

8   7)76   9   8)42   10 6)38   11 9)80

12 7)30   13 8)30   14 6)44   15 8)50

16 9)60   17 6)14   18 7)64   19 4)25

20 6)40   21 8)18   22 9)47   23 6)28

Four tyres are
put on each car.

How many tyres
are left over?

24.   5 r 2
      4)2 2

24

22 tyres

25

26 tyres

26

38 tyres

27

42 tyres

28

18 tyres

29

21 tyres

30

29 tyres

31
34 tyres

Dividing

> Eight pencils fit in a pack.

> How many pencils are left over?

1.

$$8\overline{)22} = 2 \text{ r } 6$$

 **1** 22 pencils

 **2** 28 pencils

 **3** 54 pencils

 **4** 66 pencils

 **5** 10 pencils

 **6** 33 pencils

 **7** 45 pencils

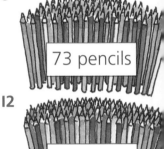 **8** 73 pencils

 **9** 59 pencils

 **10** 19 pencils

 **11** 30 pencils

 **12** 84 pencils

> Seven crayons fit in a box.

> How many crayons are left over?

13.

$$7\overline{)54} = 7 \text{ r } 5$$

 **13** 54 crayons

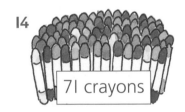 **14** 71 crayons

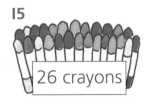 **15** 26 crayons

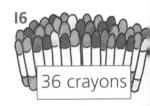 **16** 36 crayons

 **17** 32 crayons

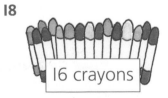 **18** 16 crayons

 **19** 59 crayons

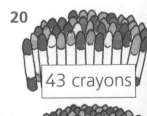 **20** 43 crayons

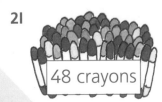 **21** 48 crayons

 **22** 67 crayons

 **23** 51 crayons

 **24** 79 crayons

Dividing

Write how many 3-hour video tapes you need to record:

1. 28 hours

$$3\overline{)28} \quad 9 \; r \; 1$$

1 0 tapes

2 13 hours	3 20 hours	4 32 hours	5 17 hours

2 13 hours   3 20 hours   4 32 hours   5 17 hours

6 29 hours   7 23 hours   8 37 hours   9 25 hours

10 34 hours   11 14 hours   12 40 hours   13 7 hours

Write how many 9-seater buses you need to carry:

14 85 children

$$9\overline{)85} \quad 9 \; r \; 4$$

1 0 buses

15 93 children   16 58 children   17 75 children   18 44 children

19 20 children   20 30 children   21 41 children   22 67 children

 Explore

Imagine your class are going on a train journey.

The children can travel in 2s, 3s, 4s, …

How many children are left over each time?

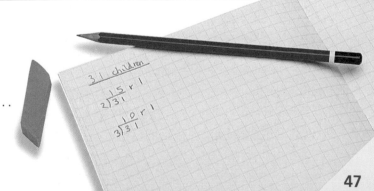

Factors

> Write the multiplications for each set.

> List the factors.

1. $2 \times 5 = 10$
   $1 \times 10 = 10$

   factors of $10 \rightarrow 1, 2, 5, 10$

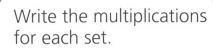

1 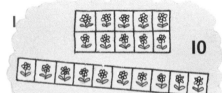 10

2 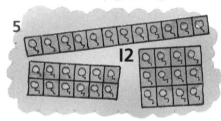 6

3  8

4 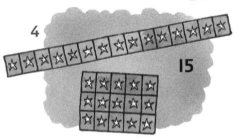 15

5 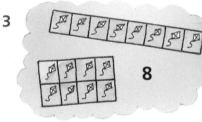 12

6  4

7  7

8 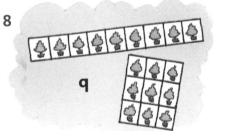 9

9 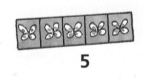 5

> Draw sets of stamps to show the factors of these numbers.

> List the factors.

10. 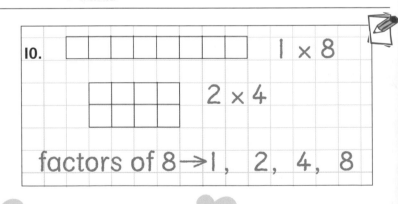 1×8

    2×4

    factors of $8 \rightarrow 1, 2, 4, 8$

10 8

11 16

12 18

13 20

14 24

15 28

Write numbers to make a different multiplication each time.

I. $1 \times 25 = 25 \quad 5 \times 5 = 25$

I ✿ × ✿ = 25   ✿ × ✿ = 25

2 ✿ × ✿ = 14   ✿ × ✿ = 14

3 ✿ × ✿ = 18   ✿ × ✿ = 18   ✿ × ✿ = 18

4 ✿ × ✿ = 16   ✿ × ✿ = 16   ✿ × ✿ = 16

5 ✿ × ✿ = 27   ✿ × ✿ = 27

List the factors of each answer.

Ia. factors of 25 → 1, 5, 25

Write true or false.

6 7 is a factor of 21

6. true

7 8 is a factor of 32   **8** 2 is a factor of 28   **9** 3 is a factor of 29

10 4 is a factor of 30   **II** 5 is a factor of 35   **12** 6 is a factor of 18

13 7 is a factor of 27   **14** 3 is a factor of 15   **15** 9 is a factor of 24

List the factors of each red number.

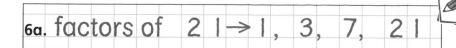

6a. factors of 21 → 1, 3, 7, 21

Factors

Write a multiplication for each yellow number.

1. $1 \times 4 = 4$

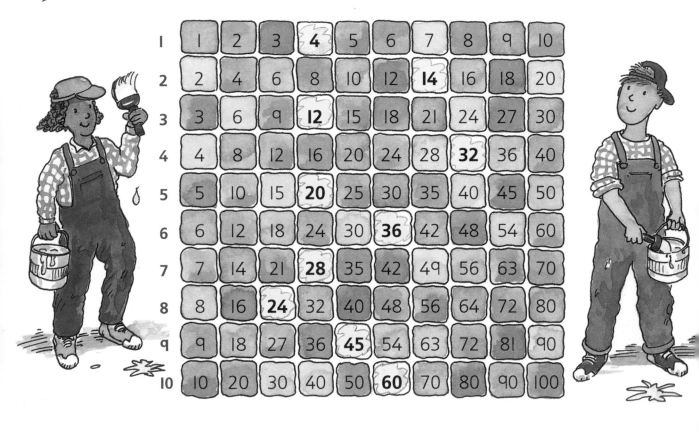

List the factors of each yellow number.

1a. factors of 4 → 1, 2, 4

Explore

List the factors of each number from 10 to 20.

Which has the most factors?

Which has the fewest factors?

Prime numbers

Write all the pairs of factors of these numbers.

1

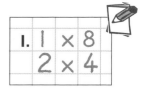

I. 1 × 8
   2 × 4

2
10

3
12

4
11

5
5

6
20

7
24

8
6

9
13

10
21

11
17

Write which numbers above are prime numbers.

Prime numbers have exactly 2 factors.

prime numbers → 11,

Copy this table. Colour all the prime numbers.

1	2	3	4	5	6	7	8	9	10
11	12	13	14	15	16	17	18	19	20

Multiplying by 10

> Copy and complete.

$1 \times 10 =$

$$1 \times 10 = 10$$

$2 \times 10 =$ $3 \times 10 =$ $4 \times 10 =$

$5 \times 10 =$ $6 \times 10 =$ $7 \times 10 =$

$8 \times 10 =$ $9 \times 10 =$ $10 \times 10 =$

$14 \times 10 =$ $17 \times 10 =$ $19 \times 10 =$

$12 \times 10 =$ $15 \times 10 =$ $20 \times 10 =$

> Each pencil costs 10p.

> How much does each child spend?

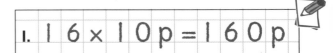

1. $16 \times 10p = 160p$

1

16 pencils

2

21 pencils

3

18 pencils

4

35 pencils

5

47 pencils

6

52 pencils

7

64 pencils

8

13 pencils

9

31 pencils

10

14 pencils

11

25 pencils

12

40 pencils

Multiplying by 100

Copy and complete.

$1 \times 100 =$

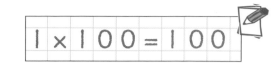
$1 \times 100 = 100$

$2 \times 100 =$ $3 \times 100 =$ $4 \times 100 =$

$5 \times 100 =$ $6 \times 100 =$ $7 \times 100 =$

$8 \times 100 =$ $9 \times 100 =$ $10 \times 100 =$

$17 \times 100 =$ $14 \times 100 =$ $21 \times 100 =$

$16 \times 100 =$ $11 \times 100 =$ $24 \times 100 =$

Write how many pence in each set.

1
£5 £1

1. $6 \times 100p = 600p$

£1 is worth the same as 100p.

2
£5 £1 £1 £1

3
£10 £1 £1

4

£5 £5 £1 £1 £1

5

£5 £1 £1 £1 £1

6
£10 £5

7
£10 £10 £1 £1 £1 £1

8

£10 £5 £1 £1

9
£10 £10 £1

10

£10 £10 £1 £10 £1 £1

11
£10 £10 £5 £1

12

£10 £10 £1 £5 £1 £1 £1

Multiplying by 100

> Each bag of nuts weighs 100 g.

> Write the total weight of each set.

1. $12 \times 100g = 1200g$

1
12 bags

2
19 bags

3
24 bags

4
31 bags

5
20 bags

6
37 bags

7
18 bags

8
30 bags

9
7 bags

10
35 bags

11
23 bags

12
41 bags

13
21 bags

14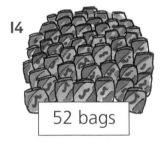
52 bags

15
17 bags

16
8 bags

> How many bags would weigh these amounts?

17   1800 g

17. 18 bags

18   2700 g   **19**   1300 g   **20**   4000 g   **21**   600 g   **22**   2100 g

Multiplying by 100

Write how many centilitres of petrol in each car.

1

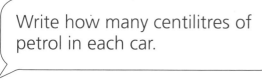
3 l

1. 3 0 0 cl

I l = 100 cl

2

21 l

3

14 l

4

10 l

5
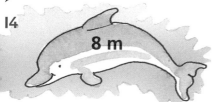
7 l

6

25 l

7

II l

8

32 l

q

18 l

10

5 l

11

20 l

12

31 l

How many centimetres long is each animal?

13
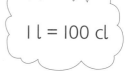
23 m

13. 2 3 0 0 cm

I m = 100 cm

14

8 m

15

17 m

16
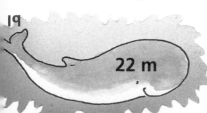
I m

17
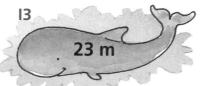
2 m

18
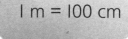
24 m

19

22 m

20
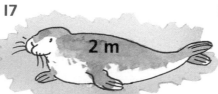
6 m

21
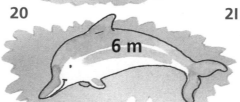
4 m

Negative numbers

Write the position of each flag.

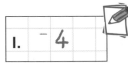

a. ⁻13

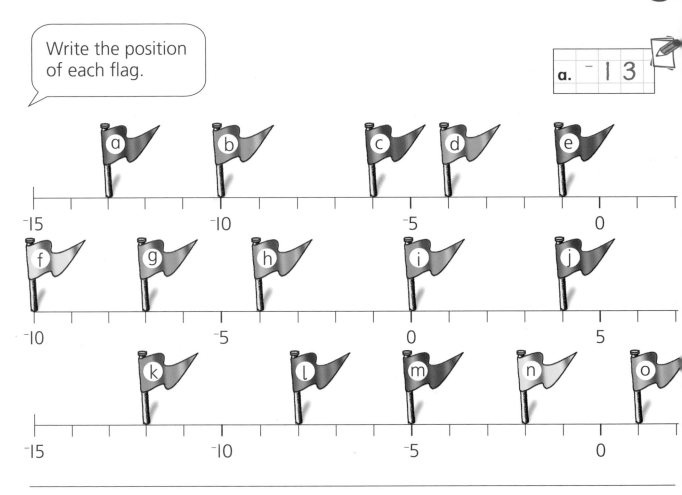

Start at 0.

Which number do you land on if you count back:

l. ⁻4

1	4	2	8	3	2	4	3	5	9	6	15
7	7	8	5	9	21	10	18	11	13	12	1

Which numbers would you reach if you started at:

a   ⁻2

b   2

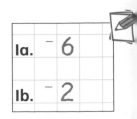

1a. ⁻6

1b. ⁻2

56

Negative numbers

Write these temperatures in order, from warmest to coldest.

27° Barbados

29°
27°

-2° Helsinki

15° Rome

0° Reykjavik

29° Perth

-4° Toronto

-1° Budapest

-5° Montreal

-8° Warsaw

-15° Moscow

Write < or > each time.

I. ⁻5 < 7

1   ⁻5, 7

2   ⁻3, ⁻10   3   15, ⁻12   4   4, 6

5   ⁻1, ⁻8   6   ⁻13, ⁻7   7   8, ⁻6

8   ⁻9, ⁻4   9   18, ⁻2   10   ⁻21, ⁻11

11   ⁻20, 14   12   0, ⁻2   13   ⁻16, ⁻12

14   10, 0   15   12, 18   16   ⁻19, 17

10 < 15 is less than

28 > 20 is more than

Negative numbers

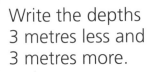

Write the depths
3 metres less and
3 metres more.

1

⁻7 m

1.	⁻4 m
	⁻10 m

2

⁻10 m

3

⁻3 m

4

⁻4 m

5

⁻20 m

6

⁻17 m

7
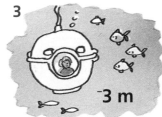
⁻11 m

8

⁻23 m

9

⁻15 m

10

⁻8 m

11

⁻13 m

12

⁻5 m

13

⁻12 m

14

⁻25 m

15

⁻31 m

16

⁻28 m

17

⁻16 m

Explore

Use cards numbered ⁻8, ⁻5, ⁻3, ⁻1, 0, 1, 4, 10.

Shuffle them and deal them into a line face up.

You can swap any 2.

How many swaps to put all the cards in order?

Decimal numbers

> Write the decimal and fraction to match.

1

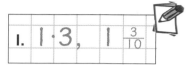
1. $1\cdot3$, $1\frac{3}{10}$

2

3

10 strips make 1 square.

4

5

6

7

8

9

10

11

12

> Draw 10 × 10 squares and colour a matching number of strips.

13

0·3

14
0·8

15
0·q

16
1·1

17
0·5

18
1·4

19
0·6

13.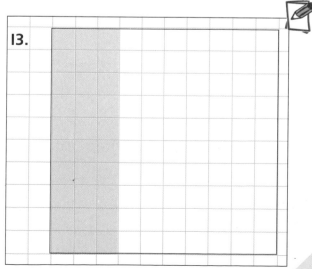

59

Decimal numbers

> Write the decimal to match.

1 5 tenths

1. 5 tenths → 0·5

---

2 12 tenths
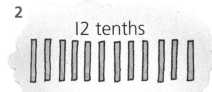

3 8 tenths

4 17 tenths
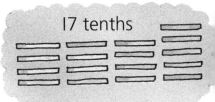

5 19 tenths

6 9 tenths
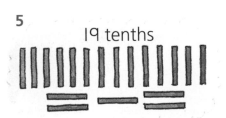

7 11 tenths

8 1 tenth

9 15 tenths
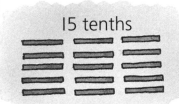

10 13 tenths
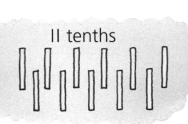

> Write < or > each time.

11 0.2, 0.4

11. 0·2 < 0·4

12 1·3, 0·3   13 0·4, 4·1   14 1·9, 2·1   15 4·5, 4·3

16 2·9, 3·0   17 3·0, 3·1   18 2·5, 3·2   19 0·5, 5·0

20 2·1, 1·2   21 0·9, 1·1   22 1·0, 1·5   23 0·1, 1·0

Decimal numbers

Write the distances in order, from shortest to longest.

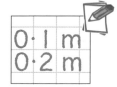

0·1 m
0·2 m

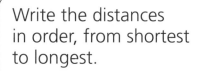
1·8 m

0·3 m

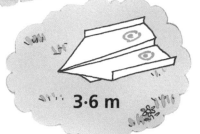
3·6 m

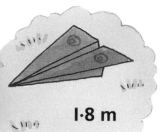
2·4 m

1·1 m

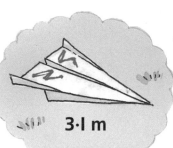
3·1 m

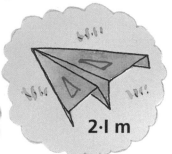
2·1 m

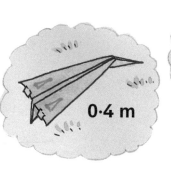
0·4 m

4·9 m

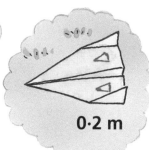
0·2 m

0·1 m

Write double each number.

1	1·1

1. double 1·1 → 2·2

2	0·3	3	0·2	4	1·4	5	2·1	6	1·6
7	3·3	8	3·6	9	0·2	10	2·3	11	2·5

Decimal numbers

Write the position of each arrow.

a. 0·2

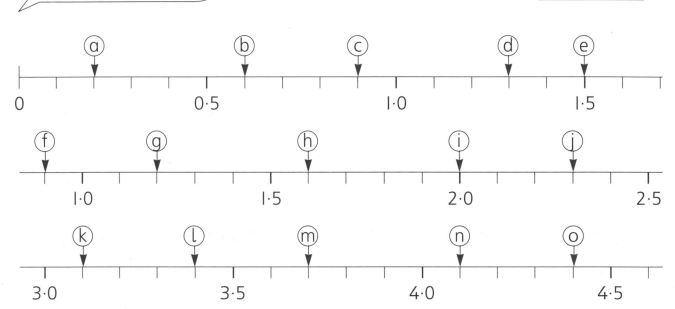

Round each length to the nearest metre.

l. 1·7 m → 2 m

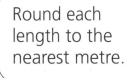

l

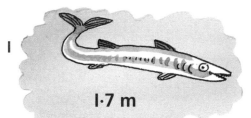

1·7 m

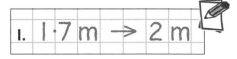

2

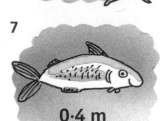

2·4 m

3

2·1 m

4

2·9 m

5

3·8 m

6

5·5 m

7

0·4 m

8

0·7 m

9

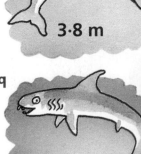

1·5 m

Decimal numbers

Round each amount to the nearest litre.

1

BROOM   6·8 l

1. 6·8 l → 7 l

2  7·2 l   TOOTLE

3  14·7 l   WHIZ

4 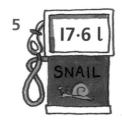 20·2 l   CHUG OIL

5 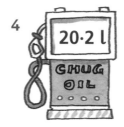 17·6 l   SNAIL

6  22·4 l   ZOOM

7  22·5 l   STAR

8  22·6 l   WHEELY

9 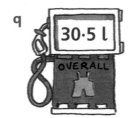 30·5 l   OVERALL

10  19·9 l   BRICK PETROL

11  20·2 l   DROP

12  8·9 l   DASH

13  9·1 l   SPLUTTER

14  15·5 l   PRONTO

15  12·2 l   DIAMOND

16  16·8 l   GUPPY

Write the nearest whole number and what must be added to make it.

17
1·6

17. 1·6 → 2
    0·4

18 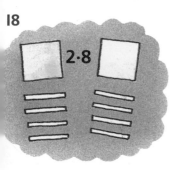 2·8

19 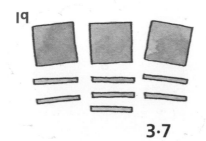 3·7

20 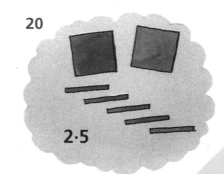 2·5

Decimal numbers

Round each distance to the nearest kilometre.

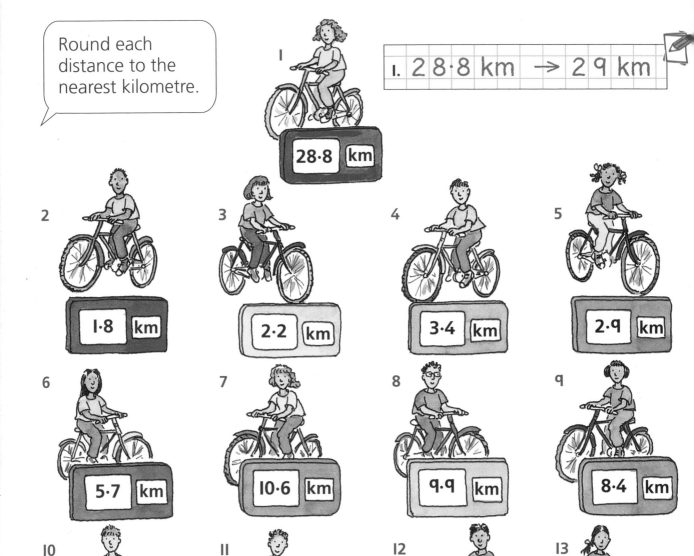

1. 2 8·8 km → 2 9 km

2. 1·8 km

3. 2·2 km

4. 3·4 km

5. 2·9 km

6. 5·7 km

7. 10·6 km

8. 9·9 km

9. 8·4 km

10. 11·1 km

11. 7·3 km

12. 3·1 km

13. 21·7 km

Explore

How many numbers round up or down to 4?

Is it the same number as for 5?